D1374391

The Goon Cartoons

THE GOON CARTOONS

Spike Milligan

Illustrated by Pete Clarke

MICHAEL JOSEPH
in association with
M & J HOBBS
LONDON

First published in Great Britain by
Michael Joseph Ltd.
44 Bedford Square, London WC1
1982

© Spike Milligan 1982
© in illustrations Pete Clarke 1982

All Rights Reserved. No part of this publication
may be reproduced, stored in a retrieval system,
or transmitted in any form or by any means,
electronic, mechanical, photocopying, recording
or otherwise, without the prior permission of the
Copyright owner.

ISBN 0 7181 2200 3

Printed by Hollen Street Press Slough
and bound by Dorstel Press, Harlow

CONTENTS

THE
LAST
GOON SHOW
OF ALL

AS EVERYBODY KNOWS, WHO READS THE 'ISLE OF ARRAN SHOE MAKERS MONTHLY', HER MAJESTY THE QUEEN WAS TO HAVE OPENED THIS GOON SHOW...

BUT, OWING TO A RUMOUR CALLED 'HEATH', SHE HAS DECLINED.

HOWEVER, AT SHORT NOTICE AND WEARING A FLORAL CRETONNE FROCK...

MR. SECOMBE HAS AGREED TO STAND IN FOR THE SOVEREIGN.

LADIES AND GENTLEMEN...

START THE SHOW...
HURRY...
START THE SHOW...

YES, HURRY HURRY.
IT'S MIN...SHE'S FALLING TO BITS.
SHE'S A LOOSE WOMAN YOU KNOW!

9

...AND NOW LADIES AND GENTLEMEN.. MY HUSBAND AND I...... ER.... ARE HAVING GREAT DIFFICULTY IN STARTING THIS GOON SHOW.

HELLO, HELLO, HELLO, HELLO?

AH! A CONS... OF OLD ENGLA...

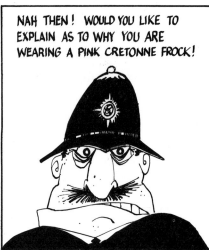

NAH THEN! WOULD YOU LIKE TO EXPLAIN AS TO WHY YOU ARE WEARING A PINK CRETONNE FROCK!

NOW LISTEN CONSTABULE.. I'M DRESSED LIKE THIS BECAUSE I HAVE BEEN ASKED TO REPRESENT HER MAJESTY THE QUEEN.

I'M SORRY YOUR Q... MY PERFUNCT APOLO...

IT'S TOO LATE FOR THAT!

...IT'S ONLY HALF-PAST FIVE?

WITH ANTI POLLUTION IN MIND, WE NOW MOVE TO THE WESTMINSTER RUBBISH DUMP, SKILFULLY SITED IN THE MIDDLE OF HYDE PARK.

TWO RAGGED FIGURES INCARNATE ARE DISCUSSING A MOOT POINT.

DON'T POINT THAT MOOT AT ME MORIARTY!

GOOD NEWS! THE COUNCIL HAS JUST DUMPED 800 FEET OF BRAND NEW LAGGING BECAUSE IT IS IN FEET AND INCHES AND WE HAVE GONE METRIC!

MORIARTY, THAT LAGGING IS GOING TO BE A LIFE-SAVER..

YES! LET'S EAT IT!

WHAT'S THE MATTER WITH YOU, YOU STUPID FRENCHY-POO? HERE WE ARE, STARVING TO DEATH - AND ALL YOU CAN THINK ABOUT IS FOOD!

13

MORIARTY- LAY YOUR LOVELY HEAD ON THIS ANVIL AND CLOSE YOUR EYES...

NOW, TASTE THIS MARGARINE....

THERE - CAN YOU TELL THE DIFFERENCE ?

YOU SEE, YOU CAN'T TELL THE DIFFERENCE BETWEEN A LUMP ON THE HEAD AND.. MARGARINE!

THE LEADERSHIP OF THE CONSERVATIVE PARTY IS YOURS FOR THE ASKING !

HERE COMES NEDDY DRIVING AN UNLICENSED GOON SHOW WITH C.D. PLATES ON.

IT DOES LOOK A BIT "SEEDY." HE'S DRESSED AS OUR GRACIOUS QUEEN! THERE MUST BE TROUBLE AT PALACE!

AHOY THERE GENTLEMEN, HAVE YOU SEEN A KNIGHTHOOD GO PAST THIS WAY?

YES! BUT RICHARD ATTENBOROUGH WAS WEARING IT...

.... AND ANYWAY IT WAS THE WRONG SIZE FOR THAT HUGE BLOATED WELSH BODY OF YOURS.

WHAT-WHAT-WHAT-WHAT? WATCH WHAT YOU SAY, OR WE'LL HAVE YOU INCARCERATED!

THE UNKINDEST CUT OF ALL!

15

NOW JUST RELAX AGAINST THIS CUT-THROAT RAZOR!

GULP

NED, ACCORDING TO YOUR MONTHLY OBITUARY, YOU WERE DISCHARGED IN 1945 FROM HIS MAJESTY'S FORCES AS A FIRST CLASS TWIT WITH A GRATUITY OF ONE HUNDRED POUNDS!

ONE HUNDRED POUNDS.. CURRENT VALUE THREE POUNDS!

NOW NED — ACCORDING TO THE "MEAN SWINE'S GAZETTE" YOU HAVE NEVER SPENT A PENNY OF THAT GRATUITY.

I'VE BEEN SAVING IT FOR A RAINY DAY

WHY?

BECAUSE I WANT TO BUY AN UMBRELLA!

HERE IS A PREVIEW OF NEXT WINTER IN JIMMY GRAFTON'S ATTIC! CAN YOUR LEGS STAND ANOTHER RECORDED WINTER LIKE THAT?

MAKING LOVE WITH COLD LEGS CAN CAUSE KNEE-TREMBLING...AND RUIN A MAN'S CHANCES IN THE OLD WEDDING STAKES.

SO WHAT DO YOU SUGGEST?

LEG-LAG!

LEG-LAG?

LEG-LAG!!!

17

19

THAT IS THE DIFFERENCE
BETWEEN MARGARINE!

BLUEBOTTLE, YOU LITTLE DEVIL! WHAT WERE YOU DOING UP MY TROUSERS?

A MAN HAS GOT TO DO WHAT HE HAS TO DO!

....AND I DID IT OVER THERE!

COME OUT OF MY TROUSERS AT ONCE YOU SPOTTY HERBERT!

MY NAME IS NOT HERBERT! I AM JAMES BOTTLE 007 ¾!

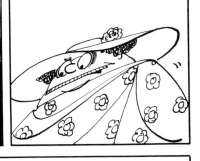

GET OUT OR I'LL FETCH YOU ONE.

I CAN FETCH IT MYSELF, THANK YOU! ..AND DON'T SHOUT AT ME PLEASE, I HAVE GOT TWO 'O' LEVELS AND A BUDGERIGAR!

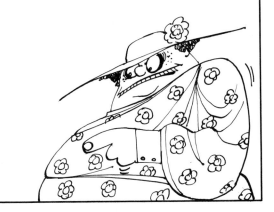

I SAY, WHAT ARE YOU DOING WITH THAT CAMERA?

I HAVE GOT CERTAIN UNSAVOURY SNAPS OF YOUR BLOOMERS.

WHAT, WHAT, WHAT, BUT, I HAVE TO WEAR THEM. YOU SEE, THAT'S PROTOCOL!

OH? WHAT HAVE YOU BEEN EATING?

GIVE ME BACK THOSE SNAPS OR I'LL NEVER BE ON 'STARS ON SUNDAY' AGAIN!

BLUEBOTTLE!! OPEN THIS TROUSER DOOR OR I'LL BREAK EVERY BONE IN MY FIST!

I'M NOT COMING OUT UNTIL YOU GIVE ME A POSTAL ORDER FOR 20 NEW PENCE, MADE OUT TO MOLLY QUOTS.

OH FOLKS, HOW CAN I RAISE THAT AMOUNT? I KNOW— I CAN DO A WEEK'S VARIETY IN MERRY BLACKPOOL!

MR. SECOMBE'S DEPARTURE FROM THE MICROPHONE IS A TIMELY ONE........ ANY DEPARTURE OF HIS IS A TIMELY ONE!

MUTTER MUTTER MUTTER

..... I HAVE A GRAVE ANNOUNCEMENT TO MAKE. JUST BEFORE THE SHOW STARTED, MR. MAX GELDRAY DIED....... HIS WIFE DESCRIBED HIS CONDITION AS "SATISFACTORY."

HENRY, MAN OF MINE....
WHERE ARE YOU ?...
... MAN OF MINE....

I'M INSIDE THE NEW
"EASY-RIDER" PIANO
MIN !

... WHICH PIANO ARE YOU IN HENRY ?

IT'S THE MAHOGANY,
LATTICE FRONTED, IRON
FRAMED UPRIGHT....

SERIAL NUMBER
935427B !

AHH ! THEY DON'T WRITE
NUMBERS LIKE THAT
ANYMORE !!

WHAT?-WHAT'S GOING ON?

BOOM

GET HER OUT THE BACK!!
WHERE'S ME SPARES? OH!!
THE LAUNDRY'LL NEVER
KEEP UP WITH THIS, YOU KNOW!!

BLOODNOK!!
COME OUT AND SURRENDER
THE FORT!

IT'S ME MORTAL ENEMY...
THE RED BLADDER!
GO AWAY BLADDER,
AND FIND YOUR OWN
TELEVISION SERIES

BLOODNOK!!
YOU COWARD!!

WHAT? HE CAN'T
CALL ME A COWARD AND
GET AWAY WITH IT!

YOU BIG
COWARD!

HE GOT AWAY WITH
IT!!!!

24

AHH, NEDDY!
NOW THEN, WHY ARE YOU
WEARING THAT LOVELY FLORAL
CRETONNE FROCK?

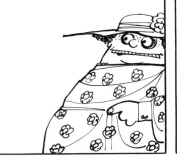

I'M DRESSED LIKE THIS
FOR GOON SHOW 161!

LOOK NED, YOU NEED REST.
THERE'S ONLY ONE PLACE,
GO DOWN INTO THE COAL-
CELLAR-DO IT THERE!

MY HEAVENS
IT'S DARK DOWN HERE.
WHAT I NEED IS A GOOD
ROYAL KIP!

I'LL JUST REST MY WEARY BODY
IN THIS SMOKELESS FUEL....
IT MUST HAVE BEEN HERE FOR
YEARS!

THERE'S NO FUEL
LIKE AN OLD FUEL!

I WASN'T SURE-BUT I THOUGHT I
COULD HEAR WHAT SOUNDED LIKE
SOMEONE EATING COKE!

CRUNCH
CRUNCH
CRUNCH

26

27

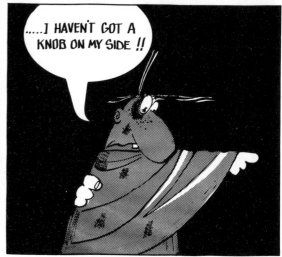

THE
AFFAIR
OF THE
LONE BANANA

THE SCENE IS THE COUNTRY HOME OF THE MARKS, MATZOS LODGE. A MYSTERY HAS BEEN COMMITTED: YOUNG FRED NURKE HAS DISAPPEARED. INTERROGATING THE RESIDENTS IS A MAN, TALL, DARK, HANDSOME, SWASHBUCKLING, INTELLIGENT........

THIS AIN'T ME FOLKS - I COME IN LATER!

NO - IT'S INSPECTOR NEDDIE SEAGOON, LATE OF THE EIGHTEENTH CENTURY AND PART INVENTOR OF THE STEAM-DRIVEN EXPLODABLE HAIRLESS TOUPEÉ.

NOW THEN MY MAN... ER.. YOUR NAME IS.?

HEADSTONE. GRAVELY HEADSTONE.

..HEADSTONE, YOU ARE A FOOTMAN?

TWO FOOT SIX TO BE EXACT.

HOW LOVELY TO BE TALL. NOW YOU SAY FRED NURKE DISAPPEARED WHILST HAVING A BOTTLE OF TEA WITH HIS MOTHER, LADY MARKS.

33

TRUE – YOU MIGHT SAY HE DISAPPEARED FROM UNDER HER VERY NOSE – IT WAS RAINING I BELIEVE.

WHERE IS HER LADYSHIP AT THE MOMENT ?

ME LADY HASN'T GOT A SHIP AT THE MOMENT.

I DON'T WISH TO KNOW THAT. SEND IN LADY MARKS !

AH, LADY MARKS, NOW YOUR LATE HUSBAND OWNED A BANANA PLANTATION, YES ?

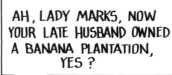

IN SOUTH AMERICA.

THAT'S ABROAD ISN'T IT ?

IT ALL DEPENDS ON WHERE YOU'RE STANDING.

LADY MARKS – THIS IS A TRICKY CASE.........
I DON'T THINK I CAN.......

INSPECTOR, YOU MUST FIND MY SON - YOU MUST. I DON'T CARE HOW MUCH MONEY YOU SPEND, IN FACT, I'LL CHIP IN A FEW BOB MYSELF.

THE OFFER IS TEMPTING. VERY WELL, I ACCEPT. JUST LEAVE EVERYTHING TO ME — YOUR PURSE, JEWELS, CHEQUE BOOK, WAR BONDS. ....

AT THE PASSPORT OFFICE, SEAGOON DISCOVERED THAT FRED NURKE HAD LEFT FOR GUATEMALA ON A BANANA BOAT - DISGUISED AS A BANANA.

MY NEXT TASK WAS TO BOOK A TICKET TO SOUTH AMERICA. THIS I DID AT A SHIPPING OFFICE, NEAR BY IN LEADENHALL STREET.

WHO IS IT? EH? WHO IS IT?

GOOD MORNING - I WANT TO BOOK TO SOUTH AMERICA.

THAT'S ABROAD ISN'T IT? NOW, LET'S GET SOME DETAILS, DOCUMENTS AND DETAILS....

... LET'S GET THE DETAILS... AND THE DOCUMENTS......... ..WE MUST HAVE DOCUMENTS AND DETAILS YOU KNOW.....

35

...MUST HAVE DOCUMENTS.....
NOW.. OH YES NOW... NAME ?

NEDDIE PUGH SEAGOON!

NEDDIE.... NEDDIE.... NEDDIE....
....WHAT WAS NEXT ?

NEDDIE *PUGH* SEAGOON!

PUGH - PHEW - THERE!
NEDDIE PUGH SEAGOON

ADDRESS ?

NO FIXED ABODE

NO FIXED ABODE ?
WHAT NUMBER ?

NUMBER 29A

DISTRICT ?

LONDON SW2

...IT'S NO GOOD - I'D BETTER
GET A PENCIL AND PAPER AND
WRITE ALL THIS DOWN !
MIN, MIN, MIN, MINEEE !

WHAT IS IT HENRY ?
YOU WANT A PENCIL ?
OK   BUDDY !

MINNIE, THIS GENTLEMAN IS
GOING TO SOUTH AMERICA.
THAT'S WHERE YOUNG.. ER..
FRED NURKE WENT TO....

FRED NURKE ?,
WHY, THAT'S FRED NURKE'S NAME !

YES, HE WENT IN SUCH A RUSH,
HE LEFT THIS BEHIND.

A LONE BANANA !
SO, NOW MY TASK WAS MUCH
EASIER - I KNEW THE MAN I
WAS LOOKING FOR WAS -
ONE BANANA SHORT !!

WITH THE BANANA SECRETED ON HIS PERSON, NEDDIE SEAGOON ARRIVED AT THE PORT OF GUATAMALA WHERE HE WAS ACCORDED THE TYPICAL LATIN WELCOME TO AN ENGLISHMAN.

HANDS UP, YOU PIG SWINE!

HAVE A CARE, LATIN DEVIL — I AM AN ENGLISHMAN. REMEMBER, THIS ROLLED UMBRELLA HAS MORE USES THAN ONE!

IT IS THE REVOLUTION, EVERYWHERE THERE IS AN ARMED UPRISING...

... NOW. IF YOU DON'T MIND, WE MUST SEARCH YOU.

WHAT FOR?

BANANAS!
YOU SEE, WE GUATEMALIANS ARE TRYING TO OVERTHROW THE FOREIGN DOMINATED PLANTATIONS....

...ANY FOREIGNER FOUND WITH A BANANA ON HIM WILL BE SHOT BY A FIRING SQUAD AND ASKED TO LEAVE THE COUNTRY!

WELL YOU MIGHT AS WELL KNOW, I'M HERE TO FIND YOUNG FRED NURKE !

THAT CAPITALIST PIG ! WHY, I'LL ....

DON'T MOVE SIGNOR GONZALES MESS, NE MORIARTY ! HANDS UP !

SEAGOON, PUT THAT BANANA DOWN !

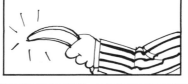

AND LEAVE MYSELF DEFENCELESS ? ONE STEP NEARER AND I FIRE !

FOOL - YOU CAN'T SHOOT A BANANA ! ILL......

SWINE ! IT WAS *LOADED* !!

OF COURSE, YOU DON'T THINK THAT I'D THREATEN YOU WITH AN UNLOADED BANANA ? NOW COME ON, TELL ME, WHERE IS FRED NURKE ?

38

I WILL NEVER TELL YOU- GO ON, TORTURE ME -
SMASH MY SKULL IN - BREAK MY BONES -
PUT LIGHTED MATCHES IN MY FINGERS-TEAR
THE FLESH FROM MY BODY -SLICE LUMPS OFF.....

GULP!

THUD!

QUICK , THE SMELLING SALTS -
HE'S FAINTED.

WHEN THE ENGLISHMAN AWOKE HE FOUND
HIMSELF IN A TALL DARK ROOM - WITH
SIDEBOARDS- IT WAS A PRISON CELL!

TRUE, TRUE. THE ONLY OTHER OCCUPANT WAS
ANOTHER OCCUPANT -HE *APPEARED* TO BE A
MAN OF BREEDING AND INTELLECT.

HELLO DERE!

I WAS WRONG — BUT WAIT— COULD HE BE FRED NURKE?

DO YOU RECOGNISE THIS BANANA?

NOPE — I DON'T THINK I'VE MET HIM BEFORE.

CURSE — THEN YOU'RE NOT FRED NURKE.

YOU MEAN I'M SOMEONE ELSE?

WHAT'S YOUR NAME?

ECCLES! — OH! DAT'S WHO I AM!

41

EYES FRONT - EVERYONE BACK TO THEIR OWN BEDS. THERE IS AN ENGLISHMAN TO SEE YOU.

ARHH! AND OTHER SUCH NAUGHTY NOISES! NOW - WHICH ONE OF YOU TWO IS ECCLES AND SEAGOON?

I'M SEAGOON EXCEPT FOR ECCLES.

I'M ECCLES EXCEPT FOR SEAGOON.

SO, YOU'RE BOTH ECCLES AND SEAGOON EXCEPT FOR EACH OTHER!
I KNEW I'D GET IT OUT OF YOU.

I'M THE BRITISH CHARGÉ D'AFFAIRS - MAJOR BLOODNOK...

..LATE OF ZSA ZSA GABOR'S THIRD REGULAR HUSBANDS. I'VE MANAGED TO SECURE YOUR RELEASE....

I COMPLETELY OVERCAME THE PRISON GUARDS - WITH MONEY!

NOW, EVERYBODY ONTO THIS TEN-SEATER HORSE...

NOWWW, GID UP THERE!

WOAH! HERE WE ARE, THE EMBASSY.

OH, IT'S YOU, SIR – AM I GLAD YOU CAME BACK!
THE REBELS HAVE BEEN TRYING TO CHOP DOWN THE BANANA TREE IN THE GARDEN.

DOGS! STAND BACK.
YOU LATIN DEVILS – BEGONE, OR I'LL COME OUT THERE AND CUT YOU DOWN!

THEY ALL WENT ABOUT THREE HOURS AGO.

43

GAD, BLOODNOK,
I ADMIRE YOUR GUTS.

WHY, ARE THEY SHOWING ?

BLOODNOK, I SEEK
FRED NURKE.

HE'S HERE TO SAVE THE
BRITISH BANANA INDUSTRY.
IN FACT, HE WENT OUT ALONE
TO DYNAMITE THE REBEL H.Q.

IN THE GROUNDS OF THE BRITISH EMBASSY, OUR HEROES
ARE DUG IN AROUND THE LONE BANANA TREE ~
THE LAST SYMBOL OF WANING BRITISH PRESTIGE IN
SOUTH AMERICA.
THEY ALL ANXIOUSLY AWAIT THE RETURN OF FRED NURKE.....

...AROUND THEM, THE JUNGLE
NIGHT IS ALIVE WITH REVELS -
AND NOCTURNAL SOUNDS ~
RAIN IN PLACES, FOG PATCHES
ON THE COAST. ARSENAL 2 -
CHINESE WANDERERS 600.

44

GAD BLOODNOK. THIS WAITING IS KILLING ME.

SHHH! NOT SO LOUD, YOU FOOL — REMEMBER, EVEN PEOPLE HAVE EARS.

IT'S THIS DARKNESS! YOU CAN'T SEE A THING.

I KNOW — FOR THREE HOURS NOW I'VE BEEN STRAINING MY EYES AND I'VE ONLY JUST MANAGED ONE PAGE OF "THE AWFUL DISCLOSURES OF MAURICE MONK", FOUR RUPEES, IN A PLAIN WRAPPER.

LISTEN — WHAT'S MAKING THAT NOISE ? MAJOR, A MAN'S JUST JUMPED OVER THE GARDEN WALL !

THEN ONE OF US MUST VOLUNTEER TO GO OUT AND GET HIM.

YES ~ ONE OF US MUST VOLUNTEER !

YER, ONE OF US MUST VOLUNTEER.

45

MEANTIME........

...ONE OF US *MUST* VOLUNTEER!

YES! ONE OF US *MUST*!!

YUP, ONE OF US *MUST*!

WELL, WHO'S IT GOING TO BE SEAGOON?

I'M SORRY, BUT I HAVE A WIFE AND SIXTY-THREE CHILDREN.

I TOO HAVE A WIFE AND CHILDREN ~ THAT ONLY LEAVES DEAR OLD........

HELLO, HELLO, OPERATOR? GET ME THE MARRIAGE BUREAU!

FLATTEN ME CRONKLER! SO, BOTH OF YOU HAVE TURNED COWARDS! TWO COWARDS AND ME. YOU KNOW WHAT THIS MEANS.

THREE COWARDS.

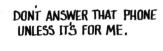

RING RING

DON'T ANSWER THAT PHONE UNLESS IT'S FOR ME.

HELLO? WHAT??? NEVER ~ NEVER, DO YOU HEAR ME? NEVER !!!

IT WAS THE REBEL LEADER— HE SAYS UNLESS WE CHOP DOWN OUR BANANA TREE AND HAND IT OVER TO THEM...

.... WE'LL DIE..... TONIGHT !!

TONIGHT? WHY, THAT'S TONIGHT !

FANCY HIM THINKING *I'D* CHOP DOWN THE BANANA TREE TO SAVE MY LOUSY SKIN ~ HA! HA!

BLOODNOK! PUT DOWN THAT FORTY-TON CHOPPER !

DISGRACEFUL! CHOPPING DOWN THE BRITISH BANANA TREE.

YER, DISGRACEFUL.

ECCLES! STOP THAT! WHERE DID YOU GET THAT SAW?

FROM THE SEA!...... IT'S A SEA-SAW!!! HA. HA!

SILENCE! WE'VE GOT TO PULL OURSELVES TOGETHER —

THIS BANANA TREE IS THE *LAST ONE* IN SOUTH AMERICA UNDER BRITISH CONTROL! REMEMBER, LADS, SOMEWHERE OUT THERE, FRED NURKE IS WORKING TO DESTROY THE REBEL H.Q. — NOW, THROW THAT CHOPPER AND SAW OVER THE WALL.

O.K!

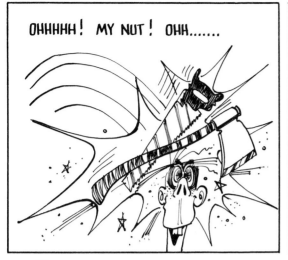

OHHHHH! MY NUT! OHH.......

I HAVE BEEN HITTED ON MY BONCE!
I WAS KIPPING ON THE GRASS, SUDDENLY~
THUD! OOOH! (CLUTCHES LUMP ON CRUST.)

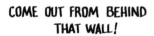

COME OUT FROM BEHIND
THAT WALL!

ENTER BLUEBOTTLE WEARING
CRASH HELMET ~ PAUSES FOR
APPLAUSE ~ NOT A SAUSAGE!
(THINKS OF RUDE SAILOR WORD)

WHO IS THIS GALLANT
LITTLE KNIGHT WITH
UNLACED PLIMSOLLS?

WHO AM I? I'M THE ONE WOT COPPED
THAT DIRTY BIG SAW ON THE NUT.
(POINTS TO LUMP AREA)

TELL ME LITTLE JAM-STAINED HERO,
COULD YOU LEAD ME TO THE REBEL H.Q.?

I CAN
SHOW YOU THE
VERY SPOT!

49

50

I DO NOT LIKE THIS GAME. I'M GOING HOME - I JUST REMEMBERED, IT'S MY TURN IN THE BARREL.

EXITS STAGE LEFT TO EAST FINCHLEY ON COUNCIL DUST CART!

VERY WELL, I'LL GO MYSELF...

... FIRST I'LL DISGUISE MYSELF AS A MEXICAN PEON.....

-THEY'LL NEVER RECOGNISE ME!

SIGNOR GRYTPYPE-THYNNE - WE FOUND THIS IDIOT HIDING IN A DUSTBIN DISGUISED AS A MEXICAN PEON.

AHHH ~ A MIDGET, EH?

SO ~ YOU'RE THE LEADER OF THE REBELS?

51

YES, NOW – *WHO ARE YOU?*

I WON'T TALK! NEVER !!

THE BRANDING IRONS!

I'M NEDDIE SEAGOON.

OH? WHERE'S FRED NURKE?

I DON'T KNOW.

SO *THAT'S* WHERE HE IS! RIGHT MORIARTY, WE'LL GO AT ONCE TO THE EMBASSY – AND BRING BACK THEIR BANANA TREE.

YOU WON'T SUCCEED ~ IT'S GUARDED BY MAJOR DENIS BLOODNOK!

BLOODNOK? MORIARTY – BRING MONEY. SEAGOON, WE'LL LOCK YOU IN HERE ~ GOODBYE!

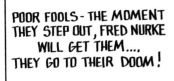

POOR FOOLS - THE MOMENT THEY STEP OUT, FRED NURKE WILL GET THEM.... THEY GO TO THEIR DOOM!

RING RING

HELLO! YES...... THIS IS THE REBEL H.Q. BUT..........

RIGHT, YOU SWINES, THIS IS *FRED NURKE* AND THIS IS MY BONANZA NIGHT! IN THREE SECONDS........ A TIME-BOMB EXPLODES IN YOUR ROOM, HA HA!

THREE SECONDS! I'VE GOT TO GET..........

OH HARD LUCK! STILL, HE TRIED. WAS HIS SACRIFICE WORTHWHILE? DID BLOODNOK SAVE THE *BANANA TREE?*

TIMBER!!!

THE
SCARLET
CAPSULE

THIS IS THE TERROR STRICKEN SERVICE OF THE B.B.C. TODAY, AT APPROXIMATELY THIS AFTERNOON A DISCOVERY WAS MADE ON THE SITE OF THE NOTTINGHILL GATE SITE OF THE GOVERNMENTS NEW 'ROADS PLAN FOR CONGESTION' TRAFFIC SCHEME....

...WORKMEN, IN THE ABSENCE OF A STRIKE, SETTLED FOR WORK AS AN ALTERNATIVE.

IT WAS DURING THE BRIEF LULL IN HIGH POWERED INERTIA THAT MAURICE ONIONS, A SCAFFOLDER'S KNEE-WRENCH, STUMBLED ACROSS SOMETHING HE'D FOUND.

HERE, HERE, JULIAN, OVER HERE MATE, HERE GET YER TROUSERS ON! HURRY JULIAN, LOOK AT THIS!

OH DEAR, SAINTS PRESERVE US..THAT'S A HUMAN SKULL!

IS IT?

IT MUST BE A WOMAN'S, THE MOUTH'S OPEN - HA HA!

SHE'S A GOONER FOR SURE, CALL THE CHINESE POLICE

57

I'M SORRY I'M LATE, BUT THE FLINN OF THE FLONN SCLUNNED THE NIB OF MY PLOON

GAD— THE HEAD OF A SKULL, I'D BETTER TAKE ITS FINGER PRINTS

LADIES AND GENTLEMEN, IN MY DUAL ROLE AS CONSTABLE AND NARRATOR, I NOW ASSUME THE MANTLE OF THE LATTER BUT ONLY FOR A BRIEF ANNOUNCEMENT...

NEXT MORNING AFTER MY REPORT AS A CONSTABLE, A MAN AND WOMAN FROM THE MINISTRY OF CERTAIN THINGS WERE FLOWN IN FROM BATTERSEA BY ROAD....

.... WITH A RUG OVER THEIR KNEES THAT TRAVELLED WITH THEM.

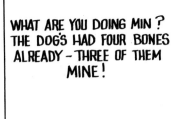

WHAT ARE YOU DOING MIN? THE DOG'S HAD FOUR BONES ALREADY — THREE OF THEM MINE!

AHH! LOOK! ANOTHER ONE. AH! LOOK!

OH LORD CRUN THIS SKULL IS FIVE MILLION YEARS OLD

HAPPY BIRTHDAY TO YOU, HAPPY BIRTHDAY TO YOU.....

THANK YOU HENRY IT'S NICE OF YOU TO REMEMBER MY SKULL.....

NOW, DIG ON... DIG ON!

MIN, STOP WALLPAPERING MY TROUSERS WHILE I'M STRAINING WITH THIS TROWEL

YOU MUST GET A NEW PAIR THEN. THE PAINT'S COMING OFF THESE KNEES

I CAN'T UNDERSTAND IT YOU KNOW, THOSE KNEES WERE HAND-PAINTED BY ANNAGOONEY

SIR, WILL YOU BE LONG, ONLY THE WORKMEN ARE WAITING TO START WORK ON THEIR TEA-BREAK

NO, NO, THIS IS A VITAL BROWN ARCHAEOLOGICAL SITE.... IT COULD BE THAT ON THIS VERY SPOT, THE FIRST MEN EXISTED.

59

MORNING, MORNING, MORNING!

OH NO!... HERE COMES PROFESSOR NED QUARTERMESS

WHOOPEE!

HELLO FOLKS IT'S ME, NED QUARTERMESS! SON OF A SCIENTIST AND DAUGHTER OF DARKNESS — TWO FOR THE PRICE OF ONE!

LOOK AT THAT !! SOMETHING'S UNDER THE GROUND

IT'S HARD. HERE, HOLD MY COCONUT TREE WHILST I HAVE A LOOK..

TAP TAP

THIS IS A JOB FOR THOSE SONS OF FUN... *THE ARMY !* CALL FOR MISS STOMACH TROUBLE 1958.... MAJOR DENIS BLOODNOK O.B.E AND BAR!

AHH! WILL I NEVER BE FREE OF THEM.... OH DEAR, NOW THEN- WHATS THE TROUBLE?

UNEXPLODED GERMAN BOMB.

WHOOSH

DON'T GET FRIGHTENED LADS. SOON HAVE IT SAFE!

SERGEANT SPINEWAIT- DIG IT UP WITH DIG.

THUS WITH TEN MEN HOLDING ONE MILLION SHOVELS THEY DUG AWAY IN THE DIRECTION OF *THE THINGGGGGG.*

AS THEY DUG THE THING TOOK SHAPE.
TWENTY FOOT LONG, RED, AS LARGE AS AN
ENGINE BOILER, WITH AN ENTRANCE ON
THE SIDE AND A SEALED COMPARTMENT
IN THE FRONT.

I DON'T LIKE THE LOOK OF IT!

WE CAN'T CHANGE IT NOW, IT'S THE ONLY ONE WE'VE GOT.

HOW'S THE WORK GOING ON THAT SILLY HARMLESS OLD BOMB EH? YOU WERE ALL FRIGHTENED OF NOTHING YOU KNOW!

IN MY CAPACITY AS NARRATOR I WILL SAY THIS: DURING THE NIGHT THOSE CONCERNED CONTINUED THEIR DIGGING.

THERE'S NO DOUBT ABOUT THESE SKULLS MIN. THEY *ARE* FIFTY MILLION YEARS OLD!

NONSENSE! IN MY OPINION THESE SKULLS WERE DROPPED BY THE GERMANS IN 1943.

UNEXPLODED GERMAN SKULLS? I HADN'T THOUGHT OF THAT.

ELEPHANT SOUP WITH SQUODGED SPUDS

I HADN'T THOUGHT OF THAT EITHER.

SABRINA IN THE BATH!

I DO HAVE SOME SPARE-TIME YOU KNOW!

62

GENTLEMEN, GENTLEMEN LOOK... FROM THE BONES WE DISCOVERED I HAVE RECONSTRUCTED AN IRISH STEW.

SO THIS IS WHAT PREHISTORIC IRISH STEWS LOOK LIKE ?

I KNEW IT! I KNEW IT! WE'RE ALL DESCENDED FROM IRISH JEWS! OI VAY!

LISTEN, SOMEONE'S SCREAMING IN AGONY....

ARGHHH

... FORTUNATELY I SPEAK IT FLUENTLY!

SERGEANT FERTANGG..... WHAT'S UP, YOUR BOOTS HAVE GONE GREY WITH WORRY !

I WAS INSIDE THE THING... PICKIN' UP PREHISTORIC FAG-ENDS WHEN I SPOTS A CREATURE CRAWLING UP THE WALL- IT WAS A WEASEL..... SUDDENLY IT WENT......

POP

63

WHAT A STRANGE AND HORRIBLE DEATH!

THEN I HEARS A HISSIN' SOUND AND A VOICE SAY 'MINARDOR'

MINARDOR? WE MUST KEEP OUR EARS NOSE AND THROAT OPEN FOR ANYTHING THAT GOES MINARDOR!

BE FOREWARNED SIR THE MINARDOR IS AN ANCIENT WORD THAT CAN BE READ IN THE WEST OF MINSTER'S LIBRARY.

IT SO HAPPENS I HAVE WESTMINSTER LIBRARY ON ME AND GAD.... LOOK, THERE I AM INSIDE EXAMINING AN OCCULT DICTIONARY....

MINARDOR? MINARDOR? M....M.... M... MIN...MIN... MIN... MIN.. MIN...

YES, YES, YES, YES, YES ?

I FEEL AN ATTACK OF CONKS COMING ON — QUICK, BRANDY !

MEANTIME......
PROFESSOR QUARTERMESS IS ENDEAVOURING TO OPEN THE FRONT COMPARTMENT.

NOW WORKMEN, I WANT YOU TO DRILL THROUGH THIS PLACE HERE YOU SEE. NOW YOU'RE SURE YOU KNOW ALL ABOUT USING MICRO-RADIUM TIPPED DRILLS FOR NON-POROUS SURFACES?

YER, YER, ALL DAT..... I KNOW ALL DAT.

OK DEN- SWITCH ON!!

65

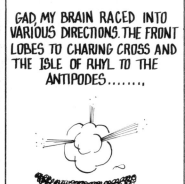

66

I KNOW WHEN I'M BEATEN.

LET ME TRY !

WHY, IT WAS OPEN ALL THE TIME !

DEAR READERS, INSIDE THE SEALED COMPARTMENT WERE THE COMPLETE SKELETONS OF THREE SERGE SUITS ALONG WITH THE BONES OF A BOWLER HAT !

MIN, GO AND PRESERVE THESE SPECIMENS IN BROWN-FUME SPIRIT AND QUILLED LEATHER.

I SAY, WHO'S THAT — WHAT'S THAT LIGHT ?

IT'S DAYLIGHT.

67

OH, LOVELY, LOVELY, HAVE YOU ANY FOOD THERE.... ANY NICE FOOD.... ANY SPOILED CHIPS AND THINGS?

WHO IS THAT?

THAT IS THE GREAT INTERNATIONAL LEAPER AND BALLOONIST EXTRAORDINARY, LE COMTE, VISCOMTE DE COMTE.....

... JIM "WINDS" MORIARTY. KNOWN AS THE MANTOVANI OF PICCADILLY.

WE ARE NOW APPROACHING THE CLIMAX OF THIS THRILLING SERIAL IN ONE PART. AROUND THE GREAT SCARLET CAPSULE THE ENTIRE CAST ARE ASSEMBLED......

MY FRIENDS, WE HAVE JUST ONE HOUR TO FIND OUT THE ORIGINS OF THIS GIANT SKRIMSONSKRAMPSON, AFTER THAT THEY ARE LETTING THE PRESS IN.

YES, HURRY UP MAN. I AM WAITING FOR A HEADLINE.

GAD! IT'S A TRILBY ON LEGS!

STEADY MY MAN. I AM ACE BLUEBOTTLE, KNOWN IN FLEET STREET AS...... 'SCOOP' BLUEBOTTLE, WONDER-BOY REPORTER.

WHAT PAPER DO YOU REPRESENT?

BROWN PAPER. WHAT IS THE WEEKLY ORGAN OF THE FINCHLEY BEAT GENERATION..... EDITORS BLUEBOTTLE & BLUEBOTTLE..... HEADLINE! BOY REPORTER BLUEBOTTLE SCOOPS. ...FROM UNDER THE NOSE OF LORD BEAVERBROOK..

FLASH!! GIANT GERMAN BOMB A HOAX. 'I DID IT IN MY SPARE TIME' SAYS SYDENHAM NIGHT WATCHMAN. SITTIN' IN HIS WATCHMAN'S HUT, GREY-HEADED SIXTY-SEVEN YEAR OLD TOM ONIONS OF PUKER'S LODGE MON., SAID 'IT ALL COME SO EASY IN THE DARK HOURS'.

69

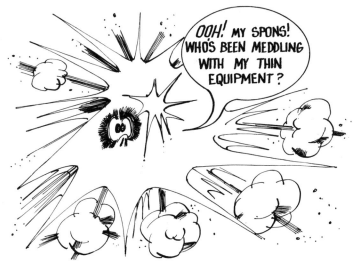

GENTLEMEN, THE COUNT AND 1 HAVE A SOLUTION TO THIS RED CAPSULE THING.

OH? HOW DO YOU KNOW?

WE JUST WATCHED THE LAST INSTALMENT ON THE TELEVISION. HA, HA!

SPLOSH

WHO THREW THAT STUFF AT THE COUNT?

GAD!....LOOK WHAT IT IS!

THE PHANTOM STRIKES AGAIN! OHH.... IT MUST BE HELL IN THERE, AND THERE'S OBVIOUSLY MORE FROM WHERE THAT CAME FROM!

IT'S BECOMING CLEARER...
THIS PROVES MY THEORY,
THE SCARLET CAPSULE IS THE
SEAT OF SPIRIT BEINGS.

SIR, THE GENTLEMEN OF THE
PRESS IS 'ERE. I TRIED TO
HOLD 'EM BACK BUT THEY
BURST THROUGH PUTTIN' MONEY
IN ME HAND.

SPOKEN LIKE A TRUE
COMMISSIONAIRE!

SPLOSH

HE'S BEEN STRUCK BY
A NEOLITHIC IRISH STEW.
IT'S THE SPIRITS AT WORK
AGAIN....

..THERE'S ONLY ONE ANSWER,
ECCLES. PREPARE A SERIES
OF T.N.T. CHARGES TO
DESTROY THE *THING.*

OH, ARHH - OOH!

SPLOSH

AHH! ANOTHER ONE!

73

ALL NIGHT PREPARATIONS TO EXPLODE 'THE THING' CONTINUED. FOR MILES AROUND, PEOPLE HAD TO BE EVACUATED.

YES, WHAT IS IT?

I'M TERRIBLY SORRY TO KNOCK YOU UP SO LATE.

THEY ALL SAY THAT!

I'M AFRAID YOU'LL HAVE TO BE EVACUATED.

OH WELL COME IN, I'LL JUST PACK A FEW THINGS.

WELL I...ER......

AT THIS POINT THE SCRIPT WAS HEAVILY CENSORED BUT WE LEAVE THE FOLLOWING BLANK SPACE FOR THE READER TO IMAGINE WHAT FOLLOWED.

YOUUU FILTHY SWINE! BACK TO YOUR OWN BEDS!!!

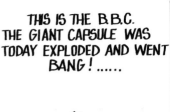

THIS IS THE B.B.C. THE GIANT CAPSULE WAS TODAY EXPLODED AND WENT BANG! ......

..LONDON TRANSPORT EXPERTS HAVE, HOWEVER, DISCOVERED WHAT THE THING WAS......

...APPARENTLY THE REMAINS OF THE THREE BLUE SERGE SUITS, FOUND INSIDE, WERE IN FACT THOSE OF THREE SIT-DOWN TUBE STRIKERS AND THE CAPSULE WAS A TUBE TRAIN THAT HAD BEEN SHUNTED INTO A SIDING AND FORGOTTEN. ...THE MYSTIC WORD *MINARDOR* WAS IN FACT THE WORD 'MIND THE DOORS'......... NOT A VERY GOOD ENDING...

MIND THE DOORS

.. BUT TIDY DON'T YOU THINK... GOODNIGHT

OHHHH!!

SPLOSH

AND THERE'S PLENTY MORE WHERE THAT CAME FROM!!!

END.

THE
PEVENSEY BAY
DISASTER

HERE TO OPEN THE TALE OF THE GREAT DRAMA IS POET AND TRAGEDIAN – WILLIAM J. MACGOONAGLE.

Ooooooooo! 'TWAS IN THE MONTH OF DECEMBER IN THE YEAR OF EIGHTEEN EIGHTY-TWO THE RAILWAY LINES NEAR PEVENSEY BAY WERE BURIED UNDER THE SNOO.

Oooo!

ALL THRO' THE NIGHT THE BLIZZARD FIEND DID LIKE A LION ROAR, THE SNOW ROSE UP FROM INCHES THREE TO INCHES THREE FOOT FOUR......, AND OOOOO THE SNOWWWW.....,

MY NAME IS NEDDIE SEAGOON, ENGINE DRIVER EXTRAORDINARY. ON THE NIGHT OF THE GREAT ENGLISH BLIZZARD I WAS DRAGGED FROM A WARM SEAT IN LEICESTER SQUARE AND TAKEN BEFORE THE DIRECTOR OF THE FAMED FILTHMUCK AND SCRAMPSON RAILWAY.

NEDDIE – LITTLE TITTLE NEDDIE, SIT DOWN – HAVE A CHOPPED LIVER CIGARETTE.

NO THANKS, I ALWAYS CHOP MY OWN !

GOOD LUCK. LISTEN, SCHLAPPER- THE LINE BETWEEN HASTINGS AND PEVENSEY BAY STATION IS UNDER TWENTY FEET OF SCHNOW. NEDDIE, WE WANT YOU TO DRIVE A SNOW-PLOUGH AND CLEAR THE LINE BEFORE MIDNIGHT.

BUT THAT WOULD BE A DANGEROUS TASK! WHAT IF I GET KILLED?

WE'D GIVE YOU A RISE - RIGHT AWAY.

BUT I'D BE DEAD.

I KNOW — BUT WHAT A FUNERAL! WHAT A FUNERAL!

GAD, IT SOUNDS A TEMPTING OFFER..... *I'LL DO IT!*

GOOD SCHLAPPER — HERE'S A KOSHER WINE GUM. OFF YOU GO.

OH THANKS VERY MUCH.

MY DUTY WAS CLEAR — CLEAR THE LINE AT PEVENSEY BAY BEFORE MIDNIGHT, LEAVING IT CLEAR FOR THE HASTINGS FLYER TO COME THROUGH.

HAVING GIVEN THE READERS THE PLOT, I MADE MY WAY TOWARDS EUSTON STATION.

PARDON ME, LITTLE LOW SUIT-TYPE MAN.

THE STRANGER HAD STEPPED OUT OF A DARK OVERCOAT — ANOTHER MAN STOOD ON HIS SHOULDER.

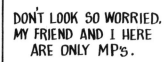

NEDDIE, MY HEAVILY OILED FRIEND HERE AND I ARE ANXIOUS TO GET TO PEVENSEY BAY STATION.

YOU'LL NEVER DO IT, THERE ARE NO TRAINS.

WE KNOW. PERHAPS A LIFT ON YOUR SNOW-PLOUGH.

OUT OF THE QUESTION. IT'S AGAINST THE RULES.

WE HAVE MONEY!

MONEY?

YES, TO PROVE WE'RE NOT LYING - HERE'S A PHOTOGRAPH OF A SHILLING.

WHAT WEALTH!

AND THERE ARE MORE PHOTOGRAPHS WHERE THAT CAME FROM.

GAD, WITH THAT TREASURE HORDE I COULD BUY ANOTHER MATCH!! NO! I WILL NOT BE TEMPTED.

NEDDIE, HAVE A HEART LAD - WE MUST GET TO PEVENSEY BAY TONIGHT. YOU SEE, NEDDIE, AT MIDNIGHT THE HASTINGS FLYER IS COMING THROUGH - ALL WE WANT TO DO IS HOLD IT UP, BLOW OPEN THE MAIL VAN AND TAKE THE GOLD BULLION INSIDE. OHHH!

STOP. YOU'RE BREAKING MY HEART - I CANNOT REFUSE SO SIMPLE A REQUEST. BE AT PLATFORM THREE IN TEN MINUTES OR AT PLATFORM TEN IN THREE MINUTES, WHICHEVER SUITS YOU BEST - BUT REMEMBER, BRING ME MY PHOTOGRAPHS OF THE MONEY.

83

Ooooooo!
THRO' THE NIGHT THE BLIZZARD RAGED.
IT COVERED PEVENSEY BAY STATION.
INSIDE THE TICKET OFFICE THERE
THE STAFF WERE IN CHARGE OF THE SITUATION.
Ooooooo!

Ooooo*!*
AND THRO' THE NIGHT, THE SNOW-PLOUGH TRAIN WAS RACING DOWN THE LINE.
A LONELY SPECTATOR WHO SAW IT PASS LOOKED UP AND SAID....

FINE, FINE!

GAD — RACE ON, STEEL JUGGERNAUT - IT'S A WONDER MEN CAN LIVE AT THIS SPEED!

CAN'T WE GO ANY FASTER?

FASTER? HAA HAA! YOU MAD FOOL, WE'RE DOING *EIGHT* MILES AN HOUR NOW!

NOW, WHAT'S THE STEAM BOILER PRESSURE? HMM-NINETY-EIGHT DEGREES. RIGHT! RUN MY BATH!

DON'T BE A FOOL! THIS IS NO TIME TO TAKE A BATH, IT'S GETTING LATE.

NONSENSE, PLENTY OF TIME. ACCORDING TO THE HAIRS ON MY WRIST IT'S ONLY HALF PAST TEN.

THE DEVIL! TAKEN ALL THE MONEY I STOLE FROM THE KIDDIES' BANK... BUT TIME WAS WASTING - I HAD TO WARN THE APPROACHING HASTINGS FLYER OF THE PLOT TO WRECK HER. SO THINKING, I STUMBLED FORWARDS THROUGH THE BLIZZARD. I MADE A PAIR OF SNOW SHOES BUT THE HEAT OF MY FEET MELTED THEM. SUDDENLY, FROM A NEARBY FROZEN POOL I HEARD.......

IN THE GOOD OLD SUMMER TIMEEE, IN THE GOOD OLD SUMMER TIMEEE....

I, SAY, DON'T YOU FEEL THE COLD?

NOPE, I GOT MY OVERCOAT ON!

LISTEN, I'VE GOT TO GET TO PEVENSEY BAY STATION AS SOON AS POSSIBLE, HEY! THAT TRICYCLE AGAINST THE WALL.... WHOSE IS IT?

MINE - A PRESENT FROM AN ADMIRER.

COULD YOU DRIVE ME TO TOWN ON IT?

OH, THE TRICYCLE AIN'T MINE - THE *WALL* WAS THE PRESENT!

WELL, DRIVE ME THERE ON THAT!

RIGHT - HOLD TIGHT!

VROOM

THE SOUND YOU ARE HEARING IS NEDDIE AND ECCLES DRIVING A WALL AT HIGH SPEED. WE THOUGHT YOU OUGHT TO KNOW. MEANTIME..........
AT PEVENSEY BAY STATION...

MR CRUN, HAS THE SNOW-PLOUGH BEEN THROUGH YET?

NO.

THANK YUCKAKABAKKAS WE'RE STILL IN TIME! FIRST I MUST GET FREE. HAVE YOU GOT A KNOT?

YES.

QUICK, GLUE ONE ONTO MY BONDS... NOW UNTIE THEM... THERE! MY HANDS WERE FREE — NOW FOR ACTION!

WHAT'S ALL THIS ABOUT?

SHHH, LISTEN — WHAT'S THAT NOISE?

IT'S A TRAIN!!!

MR SEACRUNE - IT'S THE SNOW-PLOUGH COME TO CLEAR THE LINE - HOORAY!!

SHH, NO, THE TWO MEN ON THE SNOW-PLOUGH ARE TRAIN ROBBERS! WE MUST STOP THEM!

OH, DON'T WORRY, THE MOMENT THEY STEP THROUGH THAT DOOR I'LL LET THEM HAVE IT WITH THIS LEATHER BLUNDERBUSS.

KNOCK KNOCK

IT'S THEM! AHEM!!! COME IN, NICE MEN.

BAM

YOU ROTTEN SWINES YOU!!!! WHAT ARE YOU DOING TO BLUEBOTTLE - I WAS WALKING ALONG COLLECTING NUMBERS LIKE A HAPPY BOY TRAIN SPOTTER WHEN - BLANGE!! THERE WAS A BLINDING FLASH. I REELED BACKWARDS CLUTCHING MY FOREHEAD - I LOOKED DOWN AND MY KNEES HAD GONE AND CERTAIN OTHER VITAL THINGS - YOU SWINES YOU!!!!

LITTLE CROSS-EYED HAIRLESS PIPE-CLEANER, WERE YOU FOLLOWED UP THE PLATFORM BY TWO MEN?

I'M NOT GOING TO TELL YOU, SHOOTING ME LIKE THAT.

COME ON, LITTLE TWO-STONE HERCULES - TELL ME IF YOU SAW TWO MEN AND YOU CAN HAVE THIS QUARTER OF DOLLY MIXTURE.

COR, DOLLY MIXTURE - THINKS - WITH THOSE TYPE SWEETS I COULD INFLUENCE CERTAIN GIRLS AT PLAYTIME - THAT BRENDA PUGH MIGHT BE ANOTHER RITA HAYWORTH!

THEN YOU'LL TELL ME?

YES, I SAW THE TWO NICE MEN WALKING UP THE LINE TOWARDS THE SIGNAL BOX.

WE MUST STOP THEM!!

MEANTIME...INSIDE THE SIGNAL BOX WEST OF PEVENSEY BAY STATION, WHICH WILL PLAY A VITALLY UNIMPORTANT PART IN THE STORY......

RING RING

ZZZZ

OH STRUFE COR BLIMESTONE A CROW... IT'S THE TORKING TELEPHONE RINGING MATE.

RING RING

HELLO, PEVENSEY BAY SIGNAL BOX MAN HERE MATE.

LISTEN MATE, PUT THE SIGNALS TO DANGER- STOP THE HASTINGS FLYER!

OH, I'LL DO THAT MATE.

WOLLOP!

HELLO! HELLO!!! MATE?

ALL VERY NICELY DONE, MORIARTY MATE. NOW SEE, THERE'S A BRIDGE TO THE RIGHT- GOOD, TAKE THESE STICKS OF DYNAMITE, PLACE THEM IN THE CENTRE OF THE SPAN AND RUN THE WIRES BACK HERE. WHEN THE HASTINGS FLYER COMES ACROSS- -WE PRESS THE PLUNGER!

HA HE HO HAR - THEN THE MONEY FROM THE BULLION VAN...HA, MOOLAH - APRIL IN PARIS......

CLICK

HELLO SIGNAL BOX? HELLO? HE'S HUNG UP!

WE'D BETTER GO AND CUT HIM DOWN.

YOU'RE RIGHT! ECCLES, GET YOUR WALL STARTED!

WHAT ABOUT ME CAPTAIN, CAN'T I COME IN THE GAME?

YES, ONLY AN IDIOT WOULD LEAVE YOU BEHIND.

LEAVE HIM BEHIND!

SILENCE! THE FAMOUS ECCLES!

SILENCE! THE FAMOUS ECCLES!

BLUEBOTTLE, TAKE THIS PHOTOGRAPH OF A RED FLAG, GO AND STAND ON THE BRIDGE NEAR THE SIGNAL BOX.....

... IF THE HASTINGS FLYER APPROACHES, STOP IT AT ALL COSTS!

OH GOOD- I WILL- I WILL BE A HERO! MY PICTURE WILL BE IN THE *EAST FINCHLEY CHRONIC* - 'BOY HERO BLUEBOTTLE'- HE HE - THINKS - THAT WILL MAKE MURIEL BATES RUN AFTER ME - BUT I WILL PLAY HARD TO GET - 'I'M SORRY MISS BATES, I AM A BUSY BOY HERO - I HAVE TO BE PHOTOGRAPHED WITH SABRINA....

...HE HE YESSS! THAT'S WHAT I'LL SAY- THINKS - I'D BETTER START WEARIN' LONG TROUSERS SOON.

COME MEN, WE MUST HURRY, THE HAIRS ON MY WRIST SAY IT'S QUARTER TO NEEDLE NARDLE NOO. FORWARD TO THE BRIDGE!

CAPTAIN! CAPTAIN! LOOK WHAT I FOUND IN THE BRIDGE!

DYNAMITE! THANK HEAVEN YOU FOUND IT. NOW PUT IT SOMEWHERE FOR SAFETY.

YES, MOVES RIGHT - PUTS DREADED DYNAMITE UNDER SIGNAL BOX FOR SAFETY..... DOES NOT NOTICE DREADED WIRES LEADING TO PLUNGER UP IN SIGNAL CABIN. THINKS - I'M FOR THE DREADED DEADING THIS WEEK!

MEN, WE MUST PUT THE SIGNALS TO DANGER, BUT OUR TWO TRAIN ROBBERS ARE UP IN THE SIGNAL CABIN.... BLUEBOTTLE, KEEP ME COVERED WITH THIS PHOTOGRAPH OF A GUN. RIGHT? LETS GO IN!